lonely planet

Argentina

Salta & the Andean Northwest p214

Iguazú Falls & the Northeast p145

Córdoba & the Central Sierras p282

Mendoza & the Central Andes p313

Uruguay p516

Buenos Aires p52

The Pampas & the Atlantic Coast p113

Bariloche & the Lake District p354

Patagonia p399

Tierra del Fuego p491

Isabel Albiston, Cathy Brown, Gregor Clark, Alex Egerton, Michael Grosberg, Anna Kaminski, Carolyn McCarthy, Anja Mutić, Adam Skolnick

Contents

SAN ANTONIO DE ARECO
P119

BY FELICITAS MOLINA/GETTY IMAGES ©

FARO JOSÉ IGNACIO P558

ELOI_OTORPE/GETTY IMAGES ©

PATAGONIALANDSCAPES/SHUTTERSTOCK ©